…ina,
… you for your
…erosity & heartfelt
sharing of your beautiful
gifts & your art of
teaching.
It is my sincere
hope that within these
words, you will find
some which speak to
you & rest there…
within your soul.

Love,
Jeri Glatter

Lessons from the Trumpet Vine

Jeri L. Glatter

First published by Dog Ear Publishing
4010 W. 86th Street, Ste H
Indianapolis, IN 46268
www.dogearpublishing.net

ISBN: 978-145750-559-1

This book is printed on acid-free paper.

Printed in the United States of America

With gratitude–

to those who have traveled before me.

Contents

The twelve illustrations included in this volume

are photographs of original oil-on-canvas paintings created by the author.

Each painting measures three feet by three feet.

When combined, the twelve paintings create a single image,

which, when displayed, measures twelve feet wide by nine feet tall.

Author's Note

With regard to capitalization in *Lessons from the Trumpet Vine*, some words are capitalized, which are normally not, since they were significant enough to me to be considered proper nouns.

In addition, with respect to dialogue and quotation marks, I have also deviated from grammatical standards. Much of the book's content is delivered through the collective voice of the characters I refer to as *the elders*. Therefore, rather than using quotation marks to identify their speech, I have inserted phrases in italics each time *the elders* begin to communicate.

Throughout *Lessons from the Trumpet Vine*, with the utmost respect, I have used the term "*spirit, the highest source, or God.*" My intention and sincere hope is to achieve a universal inclusion to all—*for all are welcome.*

My Intention

Facing the South, I stand with an open heart to receive any gift or knowledge bestowed upon me. I stand with humility, understanding that this is not for me alone. Rather, I have been granted an opportunity to serve.

I stand to the West and ask for strength and courage, to live my life in the manner required to remain a clean and clear vessel. Through discipline, I now understand, comes the ability to seek spirit, the highest source, or God, and to experience true freedom.

I turn to the North as I request the diminishment of ego, asking always to be reminded that I have been granted my gifts, that I should not attach personal grandiosity to my work, and that I am to remain in appreciation, as an observer.

Lastly, I face the East as I make my commitment to greet each day with gratitude,
dedicating myself to be in the presence of this great peace so I might serve the highest good.

Foreword

I closed my eyes.

The scene filled with a beautiful swirl of lavender smoke curving upward, undulating on unseen rhythmic tides, weaving up and around, up and around. There were multitudes of hues. The deep, rich purple of a full, ripe eggplant heavy on a vine, ready for harvest. The delicate, soft lilac resting upon the petals of a flower newly bloomed. Sheer veils of sultry, intense lavenders flowing in unison as they danced with light, airy blues.

I watched the smoke travel, becoming a magnificent landscape of energy cascading into grassy green valleys, inching over every blade and tree, climbing upon peaks of mountain ranges, spilling into streams, then swelling with a gentle rise and fall on a journey out to the sea.

As my view narrowed and became focused, I saw a canopy of smoke embracing *the four*, whom I would come to know as *the elders* and who had been granted the privilege of putting fire to the sage. I watched as they bowed in gentle respect and in quiet tradition and honor. Gently bringing forth their own life's breath—inhaling and then, in a release, exhaling upon the embers—they ignited new life, which grew visible in the bright orange fire. The burning sage became alive, creating an internal pulse that beat in bursts of yellows, reds, and oranges. Then the brightness of the flames quieted and receded, burning from within, as if the smoldering colors had become the fire's heart. Unknowingly at the time, I watched as the gifts of messages billowed outward in unspoken words, on pages of smoke, in a language I did not yet understand.

As I watched *the four*, I could sense that every fiber of their beings, their every thought and intention, was focused and drawn upon this simple task. Gently, they began to sway, their shoulders rising and lowering, forming hills of motion. Their bodies created a subtle dance as they mimicked the rhythm of the smoke. Clouds swirled around them, ever changing, as if in a courtship. Wispy threads and dense patches of fog formed shapes and then dispersed. Each unique second was the result of an action from their steps as they danced, or from a movement drawn from long ago—*an ancient breeze created by children running across a meadow, a thousand miles away and a hundred days before*—and now, *just now*, that echo was reaching us. All time was one.

As I looked beyond *the four*, I saw an undulating glow moving gently toward me, coming closer and closer, illuminating my face. The continuous flow was a milky iridescence, with silver glimmering points and spiraling golden dust. Every color in existence seemed to be contained therein, and yet a transparency was there as well. I watched the glow pour over me in an arc, as water pours from a vessel. While trying to hold on to the last drop of my will, my breathing turned shallow, and I exhaled the last of my resistance. In doing so, I felt the knowledge come. *I was safe.*

When I took my first breath of trust, which filled my lungs fuller than any breath before had ever done, oxygen simultaneously reached each and every cell, filling them to an expanded capacity. The closing of my eyes had triggered an opening to something new. In that instant, there was fullness overflowing within my heart. Then the dam I'd constructed to separate me from my vulnerabilities broke free, and, with a rush, a release occurred, as though blood had never coursed through my body prior to that moment. For the first time in my life, I felt joined, united. My soul, my quiet mind, and my internal voice had finally come forward to interlace with my everyday existence, and I realized that I was listening to their first conversation. My face flushed as warmth emanated from what had been the raw depths of my inner self. I was experiencing a spiritual homecoming. *I was whole.*

That was the moment—the conclusion of my seeking. The door of my soul had finally opened. The required work to come to this doorway had been completed. I had believed that, when and if this time ever arrived, my journey *into the canyon* would finally be complete. I had prayed. I had begged. I had cried out for this moment so many, many times. I had pleaded as I knelt humbled and bent, crushed with the pain of truth, unable to stand, and yet I had stood for another day. All of my struggles, all of my willingness and reluctance, all of the illusions and delusions I had created had been stripped away in my effort to seek truth.

Now my quest had brought me to this point. I had imagined that this would, at long last, be the end of my journey—that I would now remain whole, that I would be healed. But I was only minimally correct. True, I was integrated. And thus, I had finally healed the damage incurred by others and myself. What I had been inconceivably wrong about was that this would be the end—the "final frontier," as I had whimsically referred to this stage of passage in my anticipation of the moment. And yet I discovered very quickly that I was as far from the end as I could have possibly been, my long journey having delivered me instead to a *beginning*—to this opening, to this *doorway*.

As I took my first step, peace fell upon me in a gentle snowfall. I wore each snowflake knitted together as a magnificent lace shawl upon my unburdened soul. And I knew the time had come—to answer my spirit and to have the courage to be misunderstood.

My Arrival—the Greeting

For the first time, the elders spoke to me, their individual voices coalescing and gently emerging as one. At long last, dear child, we see you are ready—you have relinquished your soul. Your heart now rests, as the struggle within you has ceased. You now stand at the spiritual gateway, where you were destined to arrive. Your reluctance has been washed away by the flowing waters. We sense your fatigue from the constant strain—physical, emotional, and spiritual. You are exhausted, and you have grown weary as you tried to hold on, as you tried to direct every aspect of your life and, at times, the lives of others. You are now free to rest, child. With this letting go—with this releasing—you will now encompass more peace than you had ever imagined or dreamed of, for you now stand in the light.

We shall carry you, as if you were a babe in our arms, for you are now ready to be reborn, without the burden of self or the confinement of an ego-driven will. All that shall remain is our light working through you. You will be restored. We four elders will accompany you as we deliver you to the door of the healer. Two elders, one of the Heavens, and one of the Earth, are embracing you, gently carrying you. The remaining two elders, one of Water and one of Air, walk quietly beside you, in profound support of this moment, for the water has washed away that which has been released, as the wind has carried our message to you.

With honor and pride, we deliver you to the door of the healer so that you may begin to heal your soul. We invite you, through forgiveness, to heal the wounds that have been done to you by others. We also encourage you to forgive those wounds which you have brought upon yourself, as you enter the realm of self-acceptance and self-love. Through this, you shall be free all the days of your life.

As we arrive, with care, we shall gently lay you upon the healing table, where you shall rest in complete safety. With dignity, we shall stand upon the *four corners* to protect you in your infancy. No others will stand watch, only we, for as long as necessary. If your healing requires all the remaining days of your journey, we shall still patiently wait, in silent protection and love. We will never falter. We will never abandon. We shall never grow tired. There is no time in the healing of a soul. This task transcends all passages of time and moves from lifetime to lifetime. The path of a soul is eternal, but there is rest eventually along the way when, at last, the soul is joined with spirit, the highest source, or God.

We honor you this day, and all of your days, as we pay tribute to your courageous journey.

The Invitation

You are now ready, *the elders said*, to receive our invitation. The necessary work required of you has been completed. Everything to this moment has had a purpose—there have not been any wasted moments or unnecessary lessons as your path has been directed, as the paths of all are. The pain and struggles of your journey were essential. Your hurt has been transformed to hope.

Whether or not you accept this invitation is your choice. If you so choose, the time is now, as we have been waiting. If you answer our call, that call will be to speak. We will carve the way. We have granted you a language, one that you understand, one that is unique to you. You are now bilingual to speak our message. You have been afraid until now, but fear not, dear child. You have been given all that you need. You know our message that lies within you. Not all will understand. Do not fear those who will not understand or accept you. They too will serve a purpose. They will become your critics, allowing you to strengthen your voice. Those who are intended to hear *will*, for they too are waiting.

Our message is not new, but eternal, and always has been. We have sent many invitations, in many different languages, and, in turn, many voices have spoken. Today you have found your voice. To speak is now your task. Write your words upon paper for others to read. We know you fear what lies ahead. Please understand that the task is not too large, only requiring as many days as you have remaining—not one more, not one less—as this is your life's work. We have given you the rooster as your totem, to remind you that at night you must rest, for the rooster will crow each day to beckon you to your undertaking.

At the dawn of each day, you will start anew. As the rooster stands proud, so shall you.

With gentle love and care, we bring to you the instructions to create our invitation. This physical invitation is merely a representation to assist you in understanding, to remind you of your acceptance and purpose. There will be many days when you will become lost, when you will be filled with doubt and fear. Fear not, though. You are safe. You will meet with difficult challenges. The journey you will travel will not be along a path without obstacles. We require your strength and your courage.

You came upon the Sycamore bark, which had shed from the tree for three seasons and now four. We know you perceived the bark had purpose, and we now grant you the ability to understand that significance. The bark shall serve as the paper upon which our invitation will be written. With appreciation, we use this gift from nature, which is no longer needed by the tree. Gather the fallen bark and bring what you collect with you to the place where you rest. Quiet yourself as you take time to enjoy the texture and beauty of each unique piece of bark. As you study the shapes, sizes, and patterns of the pieces of bark, select one of your choosing. Your selection will become the paper on which our invitation is written to you.

You have two feathers that you have collected during your travels. They were placed in your path intentionally. Those two feathers are to adorn the invitation, and each one is symbolic. Gently rest the first feather near the top of the Sycamore bark. That feather will represent the wing that brings things *to* you, things that have come from spirit, the highest source, or God. Let that feather remind you that your particular abilities and talents are gifts which have been *given* to you. You must always remember that your gifts are bestowed upon you and are not of your own making. You must remain humble.

With profound intention, place the second feather next to the first feather, but lower than the first feather, for nothing is above spirit, the highest source, or God. That second feather will serve as your instruction, representing the second wing, the task of *giving away*. Your purpose is to extend our invitation to others through your written words and paintings.

Next, with cotton string, tie the two feathers onto the Sycamore bark. We use cotton, which has grown from the soil, to honor Mother Earth and to remind us to be respectful as we pay tribute to her. The act of tying together represents our love, for we encompass you and hold you in complete acceptance and love. The cotton fibers of the string have been twisted together by human hands. Let this remind you that this is where you walk. You are of the Earth, and, therefore, you have limitations. You are not superior; you are merely a recipient of your gifts—as all are. You are but a messenger. You must not lose sight of that.

Lastly, hold the sage, no longer burning, within your hand as you drag the ashes across the Sycamore bark. These charcoal ashes are the words of our message, which have been given to you. They have been whispered to your soul. Cherish these words and the gift of this invitation. Understand that the acceptance of this invitation brings great responsibility for trueness of spirit. This will require constant self-discipline of ego, maintenance of pure intention, and management of fear. You will struggle with all of these things; do not let them become obstacles that prevent you from completing your task.

Safeguard the invitation. At times you will need to refer to what you have just made to serve as your guide. When the time is right, we will ask you to share these instructions with others, so those who choose may create their own unique invitations. They shall also become messengers of our love. They too will share their gifts with others, whatever they are—for there are none without gifts. Cherish this invitation, which has been given in the purest form of love, for the sole intention of serving the highest good.

Welcome

I followed the well-traveled dirt path, understanding that many had traveled this same route before me. The vegetation growing along the path's edges guided me and created an unbroken line of signposts. A scrappy bush with thorny protrusions urged me away, as the friendly greeting of a flowering green shaft encouraged me. Each of those signposts served as a kind reminder for me to "stay on course, stay on course."

The topography was gentle, with rounded rocks jutting out from the foothills to my right. The path wandered lazily, curving to one side first, then back to the other. If I chose, I was able to watch myself through my mind's eye as I traveled along the meandering course. Progressing forward, I saw on my left a shallow meadow graced with a gathering of silver dollar birch trees. The metallic texture of the sage green leaves chimed a soft song of welcome in the breeze. I watched as the tall grasses surrounding the trees swayed with the warm air, creating a ballet. The meadow was alive with motion and movement.

As I came around a final wide sweep, my view expanded, and before me rested a village. In a central clearing of the village, a fire was softly burning, creating smoky clouds which became a roof of thought and protection. Remnants of ancient ashes and blackened stone revealed that there had been many, many fires there. This history embraced the fire of that day and served as the foundation beneath the flames.

On the ground surrounding the fire lay woven blankets for gathering. The four elders were sitting around the fire; they served as a compass for the village and for all of humanity. North, South, East, West. Air, Earth, Fire, Water. Spirit, Love, Compassion, Forgiveness. I was graced with the understanding that the possibility of balance and harmony lived within those elements. I felt my heart being drawn toward the elders. I slowly moved toward them, with hesitation, uncertain if I should approach. Their significance was reverent, and I wished to remain humble and respectful. As I walked toward them, they began to speak again.

We see you are ready, *they said to me*. You have come to the village today, as we requested. You are ready to accept our invitation. Today is the first day of your journey. You will become yet another voice in the choir. You draw pictures with your words, and you will see how those words can help others, offering peace to those who will understand your language. But you must choose this, and you must do your work. This is your intended gift.

All will flow smoothly in the stream, as the waters of your intention flow with the universe, to serve the *highest good*. This is not to say there will not be struggles. Boulders also live in the stream, but as you now move in a purposeful direction, you will overcome. You will not drown. At times, you will rush over fields of rocks with a magnificent velocity. Do not believe that you are creating those moments, nor should you attach any grandiosity, for this ability to rise above such obstacles is a gift which carries you. Learn to enjoy those moments and be thankful, but do not come to expect them. They too require effort.

At times, you will need to adjust your course, as you will be blocked by the largest of boulders. With that adjustment will come the understanding that there is much that is not within your power to move or change. At other times, you will need to flow quietly within the hidden current beneath the surface. This will teach you humility and grace. Much practice and time will be required to learn how to discern the appropriate action. This lesson will travel with you for your lifetime. You must come to the village each day. Your absence will create a dam, preventing the flow of the stream. Do not allow that. We ask you to keep the flow in constant motion. As life is ever-changing, so shall you be.

Each day you must exercise the ability to let go of the outcome of your work. This will be one of your most difficult challenges. The result is not yours to design, and this understanding requires an act of faith. You must let go of your plans and your view of what your life could be. You must trust, and work, and visit the village daily with an open heart and an open mind. View the need to know the effect of your work as an unwanted boulder blocking your flow. Use the momentum of your faith to push the boulder aside. Each push will make you stronger and more capable, until one day the boulder will rest on the riverside.

We welcome you this day. We see the fear has left you. We know your path has been long and, at times, arduous. There was much to overcome and much to learn, and you have done well. We honor your courage. We are so pleased to have you join us as we invite you to sit among the elders. There is a great deal to be accomplished. So many souls are hurting. Bring light. Bring hope. Bring inspiration.

We have formed a partnership with you, and we will protect you. We will bring fellow travelers to accompany you and help you with your task. Do not lose sight of your intention or purpose. Remember that, for all of your days, you will need to come to the village, where we will sit together by the fire. This too will become easier as you grow stronger. Love those who do not understand, though they may not be able to love you in return. Now is not their time, or perhaps your voice is not the one meant for their ears.

When you feel as though you are traveling alone, do not be lonely. We are here. We will always be waiting. We will never abandon you. Our love and guidance is never-ending and will last for eternity. However, *we* will not come to *you*—you must come to us. This is another of your tasks, and therein you will understand enlightenment, which does not live upon your doorstep but is, instead, an act of seeking.

We have revealed ourselves to you as you worked to seek us. If you choose to continue to accept our invitation, we will be waiting. Your path will be one of pouring out. We will refill you. Focus on that knowledge and draw from that power, which is yours for the asking. Walk with pride. Not all will understand. You are strong enough. Plant your feet firmly in that truth. We have beckoned you, and you have answered. We are overjoyed. Welcome.

The Elders

You are coming to know us, *the elders said to me*. We evolve in your discovery of trust. We came to you initially, as you were able to see, in images from your experiences that you could understand. As your trust grows, we will further reveal ourselves, as there is much to know. There is no end; there is only the path you travel, continuous, without end or beginning. Hours only mark the passage of time in manageable blocks—a day, a month, a year … a lifetime. Even in death, the end does not appear, for death is just another point in time. The moments are infinite, creating a circle of life, of joy, and of growth—and yes, at times, of sadness.

We came to you in a gentle image, four elders with blankets draped upon our shoulders. We were surrounded by gentle breezes to welcome you, with wisdom in our eyes and love in our hearts. Now you see with wider eyes. Look how far you have come! At times you believe that you fear us, and you run away. Your legs carry you, but your soul stays with us. We have always been the whispering song of your soul. We will never leave you. Fear not. Stop running and allow your legs to rest. Use them to stand stronger in your truth. We run with you. We dance with you. We breathe with you. You have worked very hard to come to this doorway. Enter now as a homecoming. Speak to us at the dawn of each day, for our songs will be many.

We know we frightened you when you placed the charcoal to paper as you were instructed. You drew wings, and four angels stood upon your canvas. This was not your plan. Until today, the elders before you carried feathers in their hands. You must understand that *any feather* will do. There is but one invitation, which comes upon a feather of love. We make ourselves known in many different voices and in many forms—the feather upon the cardinal's wing, the soaring feathers of the hawk, the rooster as he crows, the elders in the village, and yes, the angels with their feathery wings. We are all the same. Fear not.

You asked for a higher purpose. We heard your prayer, and an invitation was sent. Now that you have accepted, use your words and paintings to extend this invitation to others. Bring them with your hope and love, spirit and joy … and courage, for the pain you have overcome allows you to stand as a testament. When you took your courageous journey into the canyon of self-discovery, your life was suspended. You were lost, and you traveled many days. But now you have emerged from the canyon, and we see you living your life on the rim. We commend you. We honor you. We call upon you to speak. Do not run in fear of what we may be. We are what you know us to be. We are love and light. We do not bring harm to anyone, only hope. You become tumbled in our appearance, which is a little amusing! To whom did you think you spoke? The voice of spirit, the highest source, or God, speaks many languages and wears many robes. What would be the point of speaking only one language, for the faces of earth are many, and all are welcome. We offer you a choice of robes, a language to your liking, for *any feather* will do.

The Lesson of Faith

I traveled the now familiar path to the village. I was beginning to know the gentle curve and warm embrace of the course well. As I came to the village, they waited for me, the four elders sitting by the fire. That day I found myself with so many questions: Where was this village? Who was this tribe? Why had I struggled so much to be in their company when being with them offered such peace? How could I bring some of this gentle love to others and to myself?

You come to us today with many questions, *the elders responded to me.* Your mind is busy as you attempt to understand who and what we are. We saw you travel in an airplane to seek us. You will not find us with your eyes, only with your heart. The village does not exist in any one location, but rather in all places, and rests at the foot of spirit, the highest source, or God, growing abundant life in the light. The village has many faces, as do the Earth's people. One face, one village, could not encompass the enormity, which is ubiquitous. We come to you with faces you easily embrace, in voices you can readily hear. What would be the point of our speaking only one language? *the elders asked me again, repeating their question from my previous visit.* All are welcome. All must be able to see and hear us, should they seek us.

We know you will struggle. That is what faith requires. Faith is not something given to you but is, instead, an act of will that must be continuously reinforced, without end. Faith is energy, requiring thought and focus. You create faith. Faith then needs devotion, dedication, and effort to be sustained.

Keep your own counsel, and quiet the voices that surround you. Listen to your heart, which speaks for us, through you. We travel with you wherever you reside.

How can I honor you this day? *I asked them.* I feel you standing with me, the four of you, the energy of your wisdom.

Then the closest elder moved next to me and rested his hand upon my head. Pause, *the elder said.* Feel the rhythm of the Earth through my hand, for I am forever connected. Feel the calm that comes to you, a calm always present in the Earth. Someday, you will not need to be reminded to feel the calm, which will eventually become the bedrock of your life's path. Allow yourself to be escorted to the bedrock, the granite of earth. Practice this as an act of faith. Bring calm to the world and love to everyone you touch.

The Lesson of Humanity

The young man stood upon the tallest boulder of the village, his legs chiseled from his daily work. His chest was bold and confident, not from the wisdom of many days, but from the promise of what lay ahead. His strength, for the moment, was his youth, his wisdom only borrowed from those who came before him. With great pride, he filled his lungs with the breath of life, as he brought the treasured gourd to his lips. The gourd, now dried and hollow, the seeds long ago planted, had been fashioned into the pride of the village. What appeared to be empty, no longer able to hold life, now held the greatest of gifts.

Then he created the call to the village. With all of his youthful promise, he momentarily became the symbolic keeper of life's breath. He inhaled deeply and paused, holding his breath. Joy filled his heart as he embraced this gift with his ribs. His head was raised in pride that he should be chosen to hold this breath, if only briefly. He became the conduit of communication. He transported the symbolic life breath from self to gourd, and then beyond, on the waves of warm sound. He stood in gratitude.

The sound spilled into the world, reverberating from moss-laden trees to the cotton burst from the pod, resonating like a mother's soft hum or bees at work. That was the call to the village. Not an alarm, but a sound of gentle embrace. *Please come. Please come. Please come to your home.*

The sound called to everyone—to those who were at the river gathering water and to those who were working in the fields. The call went out to the ones whose jobs were the daily chores, to the fire keepers, and to those who turned the cornmeal into a gift of nourishment. The call was directed to the leaders, to the teachers, and to the healers. The call was to the children running among them, to the animals, birds, fish, and fowl, and to all who sat by the fire.

Upon hearing the call of the gourd, they put their tasks to rest. Smiles formed upon their lips, for they knew this was a summons of love. They were grateful for their ears. Those who were unable to hear the sound saw the call in the eyes of others. Those who were unable to see felt the call's vibration. Those who needed to be led were led by others, and those who needed to be carried were carried. All who chose to come did so. All were welcome. Their walk was not brisk, nor did they tarry. They came from all directions—North, South, East and West—from the farthest points of their land and from only feet away.

When the last had arrived, all stood shoulder-to-shoulder, forming a circle. The four elders gently smiled with approval and spoke regally with pride. Look among you, *they said*, and see what you have accomplished! Together we form a circle, as we represent the bowl of humanity and life. Each of you has come, and each of you has brought a portion of the bowl we now create. How magnificent our bowl! Each and every one of you—from the smallest swaddled baby against her mother's chest to the strongest and wisest among you—and every grain of sand in between are necessary. Each of you has come together with the rest to form the richest of clays, and from that unity, our bowl has been created. Our bowl of humanity is strong, and from within, we can hold the weak. We can bring forth the harvest, hold our life water, heal the sick, bury the tired, and live in harmony.

A voice was heard. What of the lost, and those who do not join us?

The elders quietly wept as they spoke again. There are some who come to the village not to live, but to continue their dying. There are some who choose to ignore the call to the village. All have a purpose. There is no waste. At times, those who remain lost lay stones in their wake, demonstrating where *not* to travel, so that others may find some grace. Whenever you meet them, embrace them and greet them with compassion and love. At times, the weakest among us are those who bring forth the most powerful of gifts. We can easily be fooled into believing that only the strongest bring us our lessons. Yet our treatment of the weak is what brings about the best in us. Their weakness becomes our strength. Thank them.

From their chests, the four elders beamed in awe and pride and continued speaking. We are so very proud of you, *they said*. Feel our pride. Take that gratification into your heart and celebrate! For this is our most important task—the bowl we create when we share the same village. All are welcome.

The Lesson of Daily Living

As I returned to the village later, I found myself experiencing many feelings and, at times, cumbersome thoughts. I was always filled with incredible surges of warmth and love, which periodically overcame me, creating an incomprehensible fullness in my heart that splashed over me in a warm, powerful wave. At times, I just needed to sit, to hold still. There were moments when I was tempted to simply rest in that glorious comfort. My inner voice stepped in hesitantly, yet knowingly, reminding me that resting was not part of my journey's purpose. Then I reluctantly allowed my logical thoughts to creep in, as I questioned the pragmatic application of how to begin living an everyday existence with this new knowledge. I was simultaneously filled with expansive hope and confusion. As I greeted the elders, they sensed my question: Where do I begin?

And then they answered. Allow us to present to you our practice for daily living, *they said to me*. Every day, as we begin anew, we must quiet ourselves. We must tap into—reach into—the life force, the energy that exists between the Heavens and the Earth. We must allow ourselves to become a conduit of that energy as we strive to do our best, to be as kind, as loving, and as generous of heart as possible.

The elders continued with their instructions. Each morning, when your rest has ended and you are preparing to embark upon your day, sit quietly and first ask this question: "How will I live this day?" This is a moment of great pause. Do not think light of the importance. Reach inside your heart as you search the corners of your soul. Feel the energy of your intention as you challenge the design of your will. Quiet your mind and listen to the direction in which you are being guided. Train your ears to hear the voice of your heart being spoken to from above. Acknowledge your wisdom, which comes from the ages and is true for all time.

Self-doubt turns your path to mud, thickening each step, making your progress more difficult. Honor your path by standing proudly in your truth. Learn to muffle the words of your critics and trust that you are being guided. Become aware that each footfall determines your integrity. Walk with love in your heart as you step with courage, dignity, kindness, and compassion.

Throughout your day, focus your attention and be mindful of your path. Look down upon your feet, for they stand only in your path. The paths beside you are not of your concern. There may be some who believe they carve your path, but they do not. All paths are directed by spirit, the highest source, or God, and all have purpose. No path is more valuable than another, for each has been touched by the same love and acceptance. There are many who choose to focus on others' paths rather than honoring their own. Pray for them, for they stand still.

Lastly, before you take your first step, drop your arms to your sides and open your hands, discarding what you must not carry. As you open your hands, say aloud, "I let go of anger, hatred, bigotry, jealousy, ego, fear, resentment, greed, self-righteousness, and judgment." These will only cause you to stray from your intended path.

Practice this, and live your life with this intention. Share this practice with others through your written word. Practice this in all of your behaviors as you live true to this doctrine. Others will view you and see the peace within your soul. Remain humble, remembering you are but one. Through this practice, a circle will widen as you move forward. There will be those with whom your words do not resonate. You are only one source of many. Do not hold yourself out for judgment *or acceptance*. This is a task of oneness within yourself. With renewed vigor, strength, and resolve, walk each step of your day with purpose, for you are answering our call.

The Lesson of Balance

Today we shall walk together, *they told me*, as we travel to stand before the trumpet vine.

Ahhhhh, we have arrived! Behold the trumpet vine! Look how magnificent! Step back as we see all of the wonder, all of the messages and information—all of the lessons. We are in awe as we look within and see how one wandering vine, one individual life force, has the ability to represent so much! We herald the discovery! This simple vine brings us abundant joy, enabling us to understand so much through simple symbolism. If we can be still enough to quiet our minds and open our hearts as we ask for the lessons to be revealed, then we are fortunate, we are blessed, and we are privileged.

You see, so many of the lessons that we speak of can be observed in studying the trumpet vine. If you were to stand before the trumpet vine, you would be foolish to believe that you're looking at a mere wandering vine, with green leaves, flowers, and pods—a vine that is simply a home for birds, or a place for bees to feed and hummingbirds to drink. On the contrary, the trumpet vine represents—as all living things do—every one of the lessons available to us.

Let us reflect upon how the trumpet vine's journey begins. Small, vulnerable, and incapable of standing alone, the trumpet vine begins life in need of support from the rich nourishment of soil, oxygen, precious water, and light. Mother Earth welcomes, allowing the roots to reach as far as possible each day, farther and farther into the soil, holding fast, anchored for safety when the winds blow and the rains fall. There will be days of storm and days of sun. The trumpet vine may not survive without reaching down with enormous strength and creating the best foundation. As the roots begin reaching into the earth, the vines simultaneously reach upward toward the Heavens, toward the light, for you see, the trumpet vine has the inner wisdom and the faith to begin reaching in *both* directions, always balanced. The vine balances the roots, creating a mirror image of the Heavens and the Earth. What is below is also above. This harmony of balance between the spiritual and the physical is one of the most universal, one of the most important, of all lessons, and you will find that lesson in all things that live, grow, and thrive. And we must also understand that humanity, like the trumpet vine, is only the energy in between the Heavens and the Earth. We are not the creator. We are not the source of the energy. We are only a manifestation of this energy and life force.

Courageously, the trumpet vine grows, the roots instinctively grasping the earth as the vines journey upward toward the light. Despite not knowing where the growth will end, the reach continues in both directions. This is the way all should live their lives. Each day, let us act as the trumpet vine. Let us look down upon our roots, hold firmly, thank the earth, and look above, saying with peace and confidence, "I do not know what my vine will look like, or where or when my journey will end. I do not know what I will come upon or what shall cross my path. But despite not knowing, despite being unsure and unable to know the final outcome, I courageously continue to grow. Each day, with faith, I will do my best to reach toward the Heavens. Each day, I will do my best to grow toward spirit, the highest source, or God, and toward love and light. Today, with gratitude, I will do everything I can to be the most glorious expression of the energy that exists between the Heavens and the Earth."

When you stand before the canvas to paint the trumpet vine—and you shall—your task will be to draw upon this knowledge, just as all of humanity shall benefit from this understanding as they stand before the canvases of their lives. There will be a common desire to look upon other trumpet vines in full splendor, which have grown for many seasons. You may wish to begin there, just as you wished to begin your painting with the strong, weathered trunk, the long vines climbing successfully over the arbor, and the magnificent blossoms trumpeting beautifully. But that vision is too soon and not for today. As you paint the canvas of the trumpet vine—the canvas of your life—you must start as the vine began, at the beginning, with humility, with the roots, and with acceptance of the need for support. Grow each day, simultaneously reaching toward the Heavens and the Earth, always seeking balance. Remember to remain in gratitude, knowing you are not the source, but rather the beautiful expression of that energy.

The Lesson of the Teacher

The next time I came to the village, dawn had just broken. Quietly, the fires were being lit. The animals were stretching as the day gently awakened. The village was lovingly embraced by lingering smoke from the fires of yesterday, and new smoke was created as the fires were rekindled. Briefly, yesterday met today, their trails entwining, representing the continuum of life. Interspersed within the gray-blue smoky quiet were streaks of warm yellow light radiating from the morning sunlight. Yesterday's memories lingered as the new day was illuminated. In the air, there was a fresh, cool dampness from the dew of the dawn interwoven with the warmth from the fires. In a replication of life, the scene contained many opposing elements as they overlapped and became history. The past floated gently away as a new cycle began. In a salute to life, the Heavens delivered moisture in the morning dew—the precious water, the life force, which allows everything to grow. The Earth gave birth again, and the offspring was another new day.

As I arrived at the door of the teacher, he was waiting there, a faint and serene smile forming upon his face. I sensed love and acceptance as he gazed at me with kind eyes filled with knowledge and wisdom.

I have been waiting for you, *the teacher said to me*, as I wait for all students of the universe. That is not to say you are not special, but you must realize that you are not unique. You are both special and not unique simultaneously. You must move forward with humility and love in your heart, always, always, remembering that your intention must be for the highest good as you learn these lessons. The lessons I teach you are not for you alone, although they will become part of you. You will also benefit from this knowledge, as will the people who touch your life and those whose lives you touch. You must understand, however, that this is not about you. You do not become a student for yourself. You become a student for all. You will share this gift of lessons in the special ability that you have, that special ability being what is unique only to you. That is what you bring. All of your experiences, what you have seen, learned, heard, and felt all now mold together to bring you, the student, to the door of the teacher today. There have been many students, and there will be many more. You are but one. Your task is to be the best student you can become. Do not judge yourself. Do not look to others for approval. Do not compare yourself to other students. Follow your own voice. Trust your voice. Trust what you believe. Trust what you learn. Trust the universe. Trust in life, love, and kindness.

Let us begin our walk of learning today. When we walk together, teacher and student, you do not walk behind me, nor do you walk before me. You walk alongside me, but your step does not match mine. My stride is one step in front of yours. This symbolizes that I am the teacher and you are the student. In this way, you demonstrate your respect of me and your acceptance that you are the student. My stride being slightly in front of yours is to remind you to remain humble and always aware that there are those who know more than you, that there are those who are wiser. Even if you were to become a teacher one day, there would always be one with more wisdom and more knowledge, for we can always learn. We can never understand all. Our task is to continue growing and learning until living is no longer.

Let today serve as our introduction to one another as a welcome salutation of the partnership of being teacher and student. Our walks will be many, as our lessons will be many. Together we will travel, as we will be met with much to learn. At times, we may join hands and face one another as we breathe deeply, our souls joining, and we will unite as one. We will merge together in understanding and harmony. The knowledge I breathe out shall become the lessons you learn. As you inhale my teaching, for that one moment, we shall become one breath. Those who teach join with the students forever in that shared knowledge. The teachers of our earth become the wisdom of future generations. They must always be honored, respected, and appreciated.

The Lesson of Self-Value

Throughout your visits with us, *the elders stressed*, we will help you understand the importance of true self-value, which is presently a struggle for you. You have created the measurement of your value through self-proclamation or judgment of your actions, thoughts, or words. At other times, you seek the words of others to provide you with an appraisal of your value. These methods are inadequate, result in a false sense of value, and are destined for failure. With love and kindness, we ask you to understand that you were born with intrinsic value, with or without your worldly accomplishments. You inaccurately believe that your value can shift and be altered dependent upon whatever you produce, create, or facilitate. This is why you find yourself requiring outside proof of your value through the words of others, or your transitory thoughts, or symbolic gain. In doing this, your self-value shifts, becomes precarious, and is subject to your most recent judgment. Your feelings of self-value and self-worth have been placed outside of yourself. This is not appropriate and will cause you to live in a way that will require the constant filling from without. You need to turn your view of self-value inward and to spirit, the highest source, or God, to equate your value.

Quiet yourself. Stop the feelings of panic and fear that you will not have something you need, that you will be without something important, or, more directly, that you are inferior. Understand, trust, and accept that you have all you require to complete your intended journey. You are protected.

If you incorrectly base your value upon outward symbols, material gain, or the words of others, you will become enslaved to those things. You will not experience true freedom. Your obtainment of material things or the voices of others will become the prison in which you live. You will be held hostage by those things. You must correct this, or you will stand to lose what you have worked so hard to attain—true freedom of your spirit and of your soul.

We bring your attention to the trumpet vine majestically draped with long, heavy seed pods that have grown as the summer wanes. Within these treasured pods are the seeds of the trumpet vines. Each one of these seeds is unique and special. One seed does not have more value than another. They all are gifts of infinite possibility from spirit, the highest source, or God. When the pod opens and the seeds begin their journey, there is no guarantee what the outcome of their journey will be. Some seeds will fall upon parched soil, and there they will remain. Some will fall, only to become the nourishment for another being, as they are carried away by an insect or a bird. Some seeds will fall upon fertile ground and begin the process of growth, only to have that growth cut short. Perhaps some seeds will not receive the required light, water, or nourishment. And some are simply not intended to grow into a trumpet vine.

Others may fall under the shadow of another vine, and within that shade, there will not be enough light for all to survive. But for each one that does not survive, another one will. Some seeds will lay down strong roots, receive all of the required nourishment, water, and light, and flourish for their journey. Others will grow abundantly but live a short time. Still others will live a very time long time, their vines turning into weathered bark. Some will produce flowers, and others will not. And some will carry forward as they produce the trumpet vines of tomorrow through the pods they grow.

Each of these seeds, despite the outcomes of their journeys, has equal value. All have been created with infinite possibilities. Their journeys, although varied, have equal value. The strongest seeds, or the seeds that grow to produce the most beautiful flowers, will not necessarily be the seeds having the greatest value. What may be viewed as a weak seed will have equal value to what is perceived as the strongest seed. At times, the strongest seed might be the one that offers hope, courage, and protection through example. At times, the weakest seed will offer life or purpose to others. All of the seeds are of service, but they are not all intended to travel the same journey. Each seed—each journey—although different, is of equal value, for each has a magnificent purpose.

The same is true of the souls inhabiting the earth. They come to this lifetime to discover and fulfill their intended purpose. Their only failure is a lack of acceptance of that purpose. Some souls want to be different than what they are, and they spend their days looking upon others, wishing another's journey was their own. This creates envy, jealousy, and lack of self-love. The unfortunate result of this is a life lived without purpose. One must find comfort, trusting that each seed, each life, has come from spirit, the highest source, or God. Therefore, each seed, each life, has intrinsic value.

The Lesson of Self-Care

On my next visit, the elders' message that followed the one of self-value began with a pronouncement that surprised me.

Today you are incapable of receiving a lesson, *they said*, as you are unable to become a student. We will assist you by providing you the necessary information, and if you so choose, we encourage you to make the adaptations required. You are lacking self-care, one of the most important tasks required to become a student. Unless you are prepared to become a student, you cannot be taught. If you were to continuously live your life in this manner, without self-care, you would become *one without lessons*. Practicing self-care to become a student is imperative. Your mind and your thoughts are distracted. Your body is tired and weary. Becoming a student requires your heart to be open and available to receive the lessons—and to receive our unyielding love and acceptance.

You have chosen to ignore the significance and necessity of self-care. You prefer to busy your actions, your thoughts, and your heart with the lives of others, even to the detriment of yourself. In doing this, within the physical world, you do not have the time required to demonstrate self-care. Spiritually, you are more comfortable if you continually look outward rather than looking inward. You hide in the care you give to others to avoid accepting the responsibility you must have to yourself. This leaves you the option of blaming others or telling yourself that you had others to manage.

This pattern of behavior will continually bring you to a place where you are not your best. When you are not your best, you fall into judgment of yourself and of others, and in doing so, you walk in anger or resentment. You must break this cycle, which has created a stop-and-start, on-and-off pattern of becoming a student, causing confusion and a lack of focus.

Self-care involves self-observation and self-honesty of intention. Self-care is required both spiritually and physically. You must continually practice the task of self-care, despite your probable discomfort. Do not rest easily and tell yourself stories for your temporary relief. You must address both the spiritual and the physical preparedness. Only through your ability to become a student will you find yourself walking upon your intended path and achieving the highest good.

As you come to us today, slumped and weakened, communicating with you is awkward and difficult. Your shoulders are not strongly held, nor are your eyes clear. You are not filled with peace, and you lack the energy and the preparedness to become a student. This is not to say that we do not love you. This is not to say we do not welcome you. This is only to say that you have not come to us today prepared to become a student. For this day, we bring you the lesson of self-care, although you will need to study this lesson when you have fully recovered. We have not abandoned you. We do not punish you, and we do not judge you. We only gently remind you and ask you to please, please become a student, for all days. Remain in partnership with us, spirit, the highest source, or God. Please practice self-care.

Practicing self-care and self-honesty is your duty and our request of you. Do not become confused. These are not acts of ego. This is not treating yourself as if you are more special or superior. This is simply caring for yourself as you would care for a child. You are your own parent, and you must care for yourself. Just as the mother would not provide unsafe substances to the child, you must behave in the same manner, and exercise the same caution, as the mother to yourself. You must treat yourself with the same amount of love, care, and protection that the mother brings to the child. Nourishing yourself and nurturing yourself with honesty are acts of self-love.

In the physical, cherish yourself by providing whole foods, which are full of nutrition. Give yourself pure gifts from the earth, presented in a safe, healthy, and life-affirming manner. Just as the mother is the womb to the child, self-care is the womb to your life. When you nourish yourself, you give birth to all possibilities for your life. Bring your body an abundance of fresh, clean water. This will replenish your cells, allowing for fluidity and motion, allowing the life force to flow within you. A parched and dry climate limits growth of plants and trees. The same is true of your mind and body. Present yourself foods that are fresh, nutritious, and wholesome. Putting poisons into your body, or eating to excess, prevents and blocks the attainment of the highest good. Foods that have been stomped upon, processed, and altered from the original source have diluted nutritional value. Bring honesty to your lips as you are providing life. This is the best and highest intention of food and nourishment, to create an environment that allows for growth.

Remember to use your physical body. The intention of our physical self is to carry us to new experiences. Use your body for discovery. Exercise your body, which, through use, creates the fuel for tomorrow.

No matter how many years pass, you must continually create an atmosphere of growth. When these lessons have been completed, there will still be more, as there exists an endless lifetime of lessons. For all of your days, even once your body has become aged, prepare yourself each day to once again become the student. That is your task. You must always provide the environment for new cells to flourish and for the formation of oxygen-rich blood, as this will become the nourishment to your organs and to your tissue.

A long and beautiful life requires new growth continuously, within your body, your thoughts, your heart, and upon your path. Always reach, to your fullest potential, within each day. In doing so, you create within yourself the possibility of becoming a student. In that way, our voice—the voice of spirit, the highest source, or God—will always be available to you.

The Lesson of Physical Self

Your view of your physical self is inaccurate, *the elders continued*, as were those of self-value and self-care. Your perspective blocks your vision, and your sight is diminished. What you believe you see, you do not. The image before you has been altered by your thoughts, judgment, and self-criticism. You are applying the vision of empty men to serve as your eyes, which remain closed to your true beauty and value. You may walk in the light on many days. You may bring the light to others on many days. But the light is extinguished when you look at yourself and you become blind.

Without proper training, you are in danger. Just as those who are physically blind need to adapt, so do you. You require information to compensate for your inability. We offer you our guidance and love. Stop looking into the glass. See yourself from within. Honor your body, the organs contained within, and the body's miraculous ability for life. Hold yourself in comfort and become the loving arms of the mother. Seek self-acceptance as a foundation for all thought. Build upon that rather than upon the hollow words of others or images thrust before you that are touted as perfection. Those do not represent our view, and we encourage you to not allow them to represent yours. Only peril lies in those perspectives. You will lay down a cornerstone of falsehood. Winds will come; water will flow; and your foundation will wash away. You will be left homeless. That is not our wish for you, or for any of humanity. You will destroy yourself through self-hatred. Time will pass, and the evidence will live upon your physical being. Embrace that proof.

Do you sit and dishonor the scarred bark and broken boughs of the aged trumpet vine? Were there not storms that raged, causing some boughs to break? Do you scold the trumpet vine for failing to have every vine and bough survive? No. You respect the trumpet vine's ability to withstand the rigors of time's passage. Likewise, so must we honor the evidence of our own survival.

You must quiet your mind from thoughts of the physical appearance of yourself and of others. You are blinded by judgment, comparison, and unreasonable expectations. Your physical self is only for this lifetime. This body, this outside shell you inhabit throughout this lifetime, is merely the housing of your soul.

We often come into our life with physical characteristics designated with purpose and intention that enable our lessons to be learned. We bring forth our spiritual needs through physical manifestations that assist us in our growth. There are no handicaps in the world of spirit, the highest source, or God. The ones without use of their legs, for example, merely have an experience or lesson to be learned, or perhaps they are to become the teachers for others. The ability to use their legs would prohibit the fulfillment of such purpose and intention. Those who are born of great beauty, admired by others, face the great challenge of overcoming the effects, and diminishing the importance, of that beauty, in order to reach the full potential of themselves. All is with purpose.

Physical appearance and physical existence are not lasting, not within a lifetime nor within the eternal world of the soul. What become everlasting are the people and situations you inspire, move, change, and create. When you touch a soul, influence a life, or teach a lesson, you change all days. And those marks you leave, if meant to be, will be passed on to another walking a similar path. Unnecessary time and attention spent merely on the outward appearance of self and others is misguided. You must monitor yourself, and this requires a self-taught discipline.

Learn to shift your focus, as if you are moving a cup of water from one table to the next. Gently pick up the cup, which you now see holds your thoughts rather than water, and transfer those thoughts from the place where they must not tarry to a more desirable location. Adjust your thoughts so they have the capacity to be everlasting, life-affirming, and fulfilling.

This continuous movement or alteration of thought will create new patterns for your mind. The more you practice this action, the more proficient you will become. You will grow to a place of serenity, peace, and calm. As this motion becomes almost automatic, your thoughts will move from a place of ego to that of the highest good. You will never be finished. This gentle shifting should last all of your days. If you are one who is able to understand and master this process, even for a single moment, then teach others. Teach them peace. Grant them serenity. Give them calm. What an amazing gift to share.

The Lesson of the Healer

On this visit to the village, I was directed to a new door, to that of the healer.

You have come to rest upon my table, weary one, *the healer said to me*. Your struggle now sleeps. I sense your openness and your readiness. I am honored and privileged to embrace you this day, to become one with you. Together we shall work to heal your wounds. We may work slowly or quickly. You may come to me for many meetings or few. I do not know how this will unfold, for we embark upon this unknown healing journey together. You, in a state of preparedness, and I, with my wisdom and knowledge, shall work together in partnership with spirit, the highest source, or God. Know that you are meant to be here at this moment, as I have also been meant to join you on your path during this time.

We will work on many levels—as the damage from wounds is complex. These wounds include the injuries cast upon you by others through deed, word, or intent. And sadly, there are also those wounds you have inflicted upon yourself. We ask that you receive the lessons and knowledge you require to rid yourself of any practices that hurt you. The intention of overcoming your wounds has directed much of your life.

Many believe they can simply bring themselves to the door of the healer and lay complacently as they wait for a cure. This is not true, for all healing is in partnership with you, spirit, the highest source, or God. I, the healer, am only present to offer my support of what takes place within you. The power does not lie within me but within you. Your intention directs all healing.

Spirit, the highest source, or God, wishes for all souls to be whole and healed. Within each of us is the capacity to be whole. The more we have healed, the greater our light, for the light of love diminishes in the shadow of hurt. Heal yourself and shine brightly, dear one.

All wounds and trauma are merely energies, but negative energies that are ultimately stored within your physical and spiritual body. Unless they are freed or released, they will be held within your body's physical, emotional, or spiritual confines. Such negative energies can give rise to physical ailments and maladies of the mind. Your goal is to free yourself of these negative energies and create space for positive energy and thoughts to enter, thrive, and multiply. Through thought and action, the practice of self-care and self-protection from others, from the environment, and even from yourself, will help prevent further injury.

At times, hurt will be impossible to avoid. Do not believe that, once you have become whole and healed, you may rest, or that you will be free from ever being wounded again. That is not true. But, rather, you will be able to avoid similar injuries from the knowledge you have gained. To imagine or expect that you would live the remainder of your days without any new wounds would mean that you would not be living life to the fullest capacity. No matter what our spiritual strength comes to be, we still live within the definition of humanity. More wounds will come. The ability to manage and recover from those new wounds is what defines your spiritual strength. This continuous healing of wounds must become a method of living your life. This awareness, this monitoring of our spiritual condition, creates the level of our serenity. This is a chore of the living. Do not think the action is unnecessary or an overwhelmingly burdensome task. This is a way of living that allows infinite possibilities for achieving your highest potential.

As co-healers, we must quiet ourselves and allow ourselves to listen. Healing is merely listening and directing the attention to that which needs healing. I offer you my hearing, as we often become deaf to our own wounds. With the deepest respect and honor, I offer you my hands, my energy, my experience, and my knowledge to accompany you in this most important process.

The Lesson of the Healing Cup

We see you are perplexed, *the elders said to me*, as you sit in confusion regarding this group of words that you have written. Despite your ability to access the many gifts of creativity which you have been granted, you still become trapped at times within the physical world. You have done much to allow yourself the freedom to enter into the realm of the intangible, and for that we are grateful. Yet, at times, you continue to struggle with what appears to be the simplest of chores, and we find this somewhat amusing. You have molded your experience with us thus far into a physical format in which you are unsuccessfully trying to fit this particular group of words. We smile at this kindly, dear one. Let us assist you.

The day that these words were written, we brought to you a magnificent vision to assist us in delivering a message. This message is our gift to the healers that walk among you, and the message also holds important instructions for them. Through this vision, we hoped that you might draw attention to the healers' unfathomable beauty and to their importance as we pay tribute to their work. We ask that they listen to our message within your words. Place this among your pages. Do not concern yourself with organized patterns in the form of chapters or prose versus poetry. All of your words are intended to serve the highest good. Stop fretting and have faith. Let the words remain as they came to you.

The Healing Cup

I saw a vision of the healer.
She stood in gentle strength.
My face flushed in awe of her beauty.
A gossamer of golden filament
created a transparent veil
luxuriously encapsulating her.
She was aglow.

Her arms were stretched open,
like the wings of the blue jay soaring,
in her welcome to the universe and
all held therein for mankind.
Her empty hands were gently cupped
in silken pods to behold
the most precious of gifts.

From her heart a labyrinth reached out—
delicate threads of golden rays.
She humbly asked for wisdom and compassion
to ebb and flow in gentle waves,
to wash upon the shore of her soul.
Her face serene in wonderment,
she silently wept.

From the midnight sky, a waterfall
cascaded upon her—
iridescent falling stars,
constellations of golden dust.
With hands overflowing,
she brought them together
to rest in front of her heart.

She gazed into her hands,
mesmerized by her treasure—
molten gold swirling in tides of pearlescent luster,
undulating and flowing.

She remained unmoving,
diligent in her task,
She asked for direction.
"Gaze into your hands," came the response. "You will see,
as cream from the udder rises from milk,
the richest of healing will come to rest on top.
Tip the cup first toward yourself. The richest is for you,
for an empty vessel cannot heal.
Practice this motion on the dawn of each day.
Then you will be able to give from the healing cup."

The Lesson of Change

Our lesson for today, *the elders said quietly*, rests in the quiet of motionlessness. We wish to speak to you of change. True change is the transformation of thought, habit, action, or belief. You currently believe that change is filled with motion and action. On the contrary, true change—everlasting change—requires the stillness of mind, body, and soul. Change occurs in our most quiet moments, as we reach into our beings and become the observers. We must study ourselves and examine our intention, along with the significance of that intention. And in those moments of quiet contemplation rather than doing, we must view ourselves with wide, honest eyes.

Change does not live upon our tongue nor in the steps we take. True change is a motionless transcending of self. Only later, once transformation has occurred, do we demonstrate our change through action. Those who exhibit change through action alone will only experience that change as long as the fuel runs. That false version of change is propelled by self-will, determination, or outside influences. True change, lasting change, must first be achieved through stillness. We must sit quietly, in contemplation, self-observation, and reflection, with stillness inside of us. We must allow our minds to view the map of our intention, which directs our actions. Upon review of this, we will see where we have misguided motives, and we will know ourselves on the most honest of levels.

You must have the willingness to sit quietly, long enough for the insight to come. This takes practice. In the quiet, you will learn to see the misalignment within. Only then will you be able to truly change your intention and thus your later actions. The misalignment of intention can be studied through observation of motive.

When you become aware of an action you believe should be changed to stop a disturbance within your life, sit quietly and ask yourself what the motive is for this action. If your motive is solely to serve a transitory need of your physical self or to misdirect your thoughts away from introspection, then you have an indication of poor intention. Next, ask yourself if the motive for this action is only to serve yourself? Is this action created solely to serve ego, material gain, or outside approval? Does this action cause hurt or harm to yourself or others? If you find yourself answering yes to any of these questions, then your motive is misdirected, and the intention of your action needs adjustment.

Your actions, directed by your motives, must have the intention of serving the highest good, for yourself or for others.

If you wish to create true change in an action, your intention is what must change. All other changes are short-lived. There may be periods of time in which you experience temporary success, but true change of your intention will not have occurred. The process of only changing the action will result in the continuance of a lifelong struggle and challenge. True change is the private design of your will.

This reflection and reassignment of motive to that of the highest good must be taken repeatedly—daily—in order to experience lasting change. We are creatures of habit and fall easily into repetition of actions. In the beginning, one must be reminded of the desire to change, and the old motive must be cast away and replaced with a new motive. This can be most easily done through morning contemplation and again at the end of the day. Some of the more difficult changes require attention throughout the day, and thought must be directed to the desired change. Oftentimes, sharing your desire to change with another individual, or aloud with yourself, can be helpful. Through the spoken voice, the mind hears and begins to absorb the change. We sit quietly here today to demonstrate self-reflection and self-observation as we practice true change of self for the highest good. This is the lesson for this day.

The Lesson of Judgment

My heart was heavy as I traveled to the village, contemplating the judgmental thoughts of others—and, at times, myself. I was curious to understand the difference between observing others' actions through three different perspectives. The first would be for the purpose of obtaining knowledge that would help with self-protection. The second would be to facilitate self-discovery. And the third perspective would be simply sitting in judgment of others as a practice or habit. I saw the negative effects of judgment, and I wished to understand the nuances of judgment. I came seeking the wisdom of the elders for guidance, direction, and insight.

Many step rapidly into the role of judgment, *the elders explained*, as a means of providing a mirror to their liking. Rather than using self-honesty and looking into the clear glass of self-observation, as the window into their soul, they prefer to use their judgment of others to serve as their mirrors to approve of their own actions and beliefs. Not only does this allow for misrepresentation, but also, our personal desires often create inaccurate shortcuts to conclusions. This practice is an easy and effortless means of self-evaluation, and since the actions of others are most usually viewed in the negative, this is a way to ensure a positive result of self-reflection. Many spend their lives in this simplistic version of self-awareness. We offer to you the awareness of seeking self-appraisal through the glass of self-reflection rather than this fabricated mirror. We ask that you leave your judgments of others, which are not intended for self-protection, on the outside doorstep of your home, to be swept away by the winds of understanding, compassion, acceptance, and love.

We wish to speak to another possibility of judgment—that judgment of others can be a disguised version of self-centeredness. By rationalizing that the actions of another person are unacceptable, one is set free, through that judgment, from interacting on a deeper level. When you do not take the time to understand or have compassion for a need someone may have of you, there is an implied permission to remain self-focused. According to that perception, you are not responsible to interact when another's thoughts, insights, or needs are deemed inappropriate by you. We offer our gentle observation that this behavior is, in the purest form, a bit lazy while enabling self-centeredness to flourish.

When one has some measure of wisdom and experience—as all do—as well as intellect and analytical capabilities in many areas or a few, then not sharing those gifts is an affront or misuse of what has been so generously granted to you. This is not to say we expect you to involuntarily expound to all, but rather to stay alert, please, when we bring someone to your doorstep. Your gifts are an extension of our love, and we often rely on those who are earthbound to assist us in aiding others. We bring to your doorstep those we love—so they may reap benefits from exposure to your abilities. Please allow this door to remain open.

Gently, with love in our hearts, we ask you to please think larger. You are so capable of seeing the broader scope of the life offered to you. Please do not be so stingy with what sprit, the highest source, or God, has so generously gifted to you. Share your bountiful gifts.

The Lesson of Self-Forgiveness

Dear child, *the elders said lovingly*, we see the sadness you are experiencing and the pressing weight of your new awareness. Despite the understanding and the grace you now encompass through our lessons, we see there now exists a newfound heartache. You have become melancholy as you pause reflectively with new eyes, as you review your past behaviors and intentions. You now see clearly the results which were directed by your previous viewpoints and your past actions and words. On one hand, your fresh perspective had made you buoyant with hope for future days. Yet you also understand the challenge and diligence which will be required of you. Through this new window, you now see clearly your past transgressions, and this is not something you had anticipated. Consequently, you now find yourself disheartened, and your soul is heavy.

Let us commend you for your insight, for reflecting upon yesterday through the eyes of your new knowledge. Moving forward with renewed grace and with good intention toward tomorrow would be far easier without this burdensome review of the debris you left behind. We understand that the path is more difficult to travel when one brings forth the knowledge of poor actions and misguided intentions into the light. We further sense your question that asks, "Now that I understand, how will I live peacefully, accepting that there have been actions which I regret, which I understand were poor, and knowing that there have been those who have been hurt by me?"

With a gentle, symbolic hand, we reach down as we compassionately raise your head. Dear child, do not look down in shame. Walking in your newly realized self-disappointment serves no one—not you, not those you have hurt, nor those whose lives you now touch. Shame and guilt serve no one. This is not our wish for you. Within the feelings of shame, regret, and guilt, the seeds of change cannot be born. Do not tarry there. Instead, we ask you to bravely take action, first through your thoughts. Learn from your errors. Study them with an open heart. Allow them to teach you where you had become misguided. In that way, you will bring forth into tomorrow the knowledge to prevent further poor actions or harmful words.

To forget about your past actions, or to allow yourself the unacceptable excuse of focusing solely on the actions of others who were in relationship with you, will prevent you from altering future behavior. Instead, allow the past to become a course of study upon which you reflect and learn for the life yet ahead. In addition, stay alert to the opportunity to correct hurt that you have caused. At times, you will be presented with a person whose path will cross yours once again. As you now stand in the light of understanding and good intention, share that light, dear child. When appropriate, share your regret with them for your actions or your words by saying to them, "I regret my actions which caused you hurt. I now fully understand the error of my deeds. I have learned from this, and I am committed to never repeat that damage again."

The most powerful way to move forward is to not allow the indulgence of self-regret but to take action that will alter your future behavior. When appropriate, share your lessons and your mistakes with those who travel next to you. Allow your transgressions to become the positive actions of others through the generosity of sharing of your darkest stories. This is the only way to transform poor past actions into future good actions by yourself and others.

The Lesson of Self-Protection

You come to the village hastily today, *the elders said*, with agitation surrounding your heart. Peace does not embrace you. Rocks have been littered upon your path, disrespectfully strewn. We feel your anger. These are not boulders whose time has come to tumble from the mountain. Nor do they create obstacles which have been placed upon your path with good intention. Their purpose is not to serve you, to teach you to *side-step* as you learn the lesson of acceptance, or to demonstrate the ability to *climb over* as you become stronger. No, this landfall is not of spirit, the highest source, God, or of nature, but of human will. We feel your discomfort. We must warn you—you have been confronted by a man of war.

Despite his days, he carries forth not wisdom but ego into each dawn, for he is *one without lessons*. His actions and words are a destructive earthquake created by his self-will, in his attempt to maneuver that which is around him. He lacks the knowledge and understanding that very little is actually within his right or ability to control. This is against all of nature and does not create harmony or balance. His behavior is in opposition to love, kindness, and goodness.

He throws rocks at those who live around him. This is by his design. He watches and waits. Just as their footfall touches their path, he acts, allowing for no preparation. Even a storm gives advance warning. He does not. This is his tactic. He hunts within his village; all that are near are his prey. No one is exempt, not even his closest allies. Do not feel safe on windless days nor with the soft outreach of his hand, for he always shows only one hand. With the other, he conceals his weapon. Do not fool yourself into believing you can be prepared, for nothing about him or what he manifests can be learned. His motives shift. His actions are unpredictable. There are no methods, no rules. In his continuous attempt to control, he becomes the volatile tornado on the open plain. You must always remain diligent and alert, using caution.

He lives in fear of the setting sun, for he knows he is one without spirit, the highest source, or God. He builds great monuments to his honor and decorates his body. This is all to disguise his image in the pond. He does this to fool himself into believing that the way he behaves is always of others' making. He believes his lies, and he rests comfortably within them. Do not let his mastery of creating those lies become interspersed with your truth. His words often contain elements of truth. Do not allow this to confuse you. His inability to be honest with *himself* is what creates his danger.

You must not join him in the moments of his frolicking dance, for that dance is short-lived and serves to mask his anger.

Should you accompany him, you will only become a mirror for his destruction. To remind yourself, hold your hands over your heart in self-protection. Shield yourself from his words, understanding that you have the power to distance your soul, if not your ears. As you quiet his voice, clear yourself of his residue. Do not let those dregs resonate in your thoughts. When you are able, clear your path of his presence. You must remain vigilant; view all interactions with him knowing that you have two separate paths. He has only attempted to come to yours. He cannot alter your direction or purpose, unless you choose to abandon your path and join him on his.

We understand your agitation. We offer you protection. Let your anger dissipate. Fear not. He has no power over your intention. He may steal your bread, but not your soul.

The Lesson of Trust

The elders cautioned me on my next visit. Notwithstanding your trepidation, *they said*, given your experience with such a man of war, we are compelled to tell you that you will become like a blindfolded child, if you do not allow some measure of trust. That trust must certainly be *guarded*, accompanied by your acceptance of the fact that, at times, you might again be met with hurt. Your experiences are not great enough to protect you from all, and without any measure of trust, there will be moments when your eyes are masked, leaving you unable to see or to make judgments where your safety is concerned. We ask you to quiet yourself and reflect upon how very small, frightened, and alone you feel at this moment. You are the abandoned child, forever the orphan, traveling with the weight of disappointment, discouragement, and defeat upon your shoulders.

Please understand that, as you travel your life's path, you can never know every element of a lifetime nor can you ever fully understand the actions of others. There is bound to be hurt. There is no perfect protection to be achieved. Striving to completely and always protect yourself is a futile task. There are lessons to be learned as you travel, and we ask you to work hard to learn them when they are presented to you. Equally as important is to accept the knowledge that there will still be unlearned lessons when you reach your last day. If you believe you will meet with only success, or that you will find yourself at the conclusion of this lifetime with the ability to be unhurt, or that all lessons will be learned, then you are preparing for disappointment. Your days will be marked by fatigue if you attempt to live a life without experiencing hurt, like the child who promises not to cry and falls asleep exhausted with a tear-stained face.

We note your intense and diligent study of your lessons and, at times, the closure of your heart, as you attempt to live a life without pain. With so much focus and energy placed upon closing, protecting, and distancing yourself, you will find very little time or space left for joy. You are the industrious watchman standing at attention at the gate of your heart and soul. You prevent entry as best as you can, and when the breach occurs, you hang your head in perceived failure. But bear in mind that, on each occasion when you prevent entry, you also block openness. And that is a perfect example of the negative effects that can accumulate when you lack trust.

Your understanding of trust is referenced as trusting people, events, or situations that arise. Yet the aspect of trust which you lack is far greater than that of where your steps fall. The trust *we* speak of rests in the Heavens, with spirit, the highest source, or God. This form of trust transcends all life circumstances and all lives. The trust we speak of involves the *process*—the experience of living—the trust in spirit, the highest source, or God, and in the guidance of what we can never fully understand.

When you find yourself at these painful moments, do not assume the occurrence rests solely within your responsibility. This is what most people tend to do. With their heads dropped in hurt and disappointment, they proceed to scold the child-self. This only compounds the pain. This practice must be avoided. When the world hurts you—something that is inevitable—become the loving caregiver to yourself. Gently brush away the tears of hurt quietly and do not let those tears dry into trails of shame to remain upon your heart or soul. Shame serves no useful purpose, must always be avoided, and never self-applied or accepted from others. With the kindest bravery, reflect and examine if a lesson waiting to be learned might be interlaced with your disappointment. Accept that aspect. You must take the risk to trust. You must experience hurt. You must learn and you must grow. You must live your life. And, in that life, joy and sorrow exist. Trust that you will find both.

The Lesson of the Fisherman

As I arrived at the village, I was greeted once again with the elders' collective voice floating upon currents of love.

This day, *they said to me*, follow us to the river to observe the fisherman at work, for his lessons are many. Walk with us in quiet gratitude for all we have been granted. We must be thankful for the blessings of our home—this place we call earth—for those blessings are plentiful and nourish us. Care must be given to never take more than we require. Do not rob, waste, or damage. Whatever we take, we must return, for our home is a complete circle of life. What we pour into the earth becomes what we live upon. We are only the temporary keepers of this home. We must always leave the future seeds for our children and future generations.

Observe the fisherman as he meticulously works, quietly and alone. On some days, in his shadow, stands the child to whom he whispers the secrets he was once taught. Always, when the time to travel to the river has come, the child accompanies him. This sacred act is never to be done alone, for tomorrow must always be honored and protected.

Watch quietly and see how his self-discipline creates a dance of rhythm and flow. In his fluid motions, he resembles the water. The gentle breezes that accompany him have become the tempo for his songs. His movements are so consistent and measured that they are almost still. Faced with the winds blowing around him, he remains calm and steadfast. He is the fisherman of the village.

He ventures into the marsh, where the tall grasses and willows grow. He wades in the cool water flowing just below his knees. He is tall, as will be the ones who follow and as are those who came before him. To everything, there is a purpose. Nothing is by accident, for all is by design. Beneath the surface of the water, the current is strong and rushes against the muscles in his legs. This is why he must be strong. Despite the forces around him, he remains steady, for he has been taught the discipline of quiet inner strength and devotion to his duty. He is one of honor, dignity, strength, and responsibility.

He bends gently as he selects thin, long, flexible green reeds to pick. His body mirrors that of the reeds he selects, he and they appearing to be one as he joins them in harmony. He has been taught how many he requires to create his basket, and he never takes more, for nothing is to be wasted. With care, he rests the reeds in the cotton hammock he wears upon his shoulder. He is thankful as he departs, knowing there will be more days of growth and warmth in the sun. He will return again when the time has come to make a new basket.

Silently, he returns to the village. Now is not the time for celebration, for this familiar task has only begun once again. He cherishes each of the reeds and keeps them moist in a bowl of river water so they will remain flexible, allowing him to fashion his basket in the days to come. His next task is to venture into the forest as he walks with his stick in his hand. He carries the stick not for hunting but to honor the strength of the branch. He will find four more. He knows that the length required is the same as his arm. He searches for only those branches which have fallen from the tree, as they are no longer needed by the tree to hold the leaves. Sometimes he travels far and sometimes near, until he finds one for each side of the basket. He knows each must be strong enough to support the weight of the fish. His basket will have four sides—North and South, East and West; Mountain and River, Sunrise and Sunset. Once he has found the four branches, he returns again to the village.

The sunrise greets him on the day he is to begin the basket. He always begins his task at dawn, as he is one of the first to arise each day. He often works in the quiet of the dawn, alone, for his task represents the sacred act of nourishment. He unfolds a soft cotton blanket upon the ground and, kneeling, arranges the four branches. From his bowl, he removes the moist reeds one at a time. He begins his pattern—Mountain to River, Mountain to River, Sunrise to Sunset, Sunrise to Sunset. As he gently weaves his basket, he quenches the reeds' thirst, dampening them as he works. The basket must remain pliable, having come from the water and needing to return to the water to perform the required task of serving as an invitation to the fish. Those fish whose time has come will swim into the basket and become nourishment for the people of the village.

When the fisherman's basket is complete, the child accompanies the fisherman to the river with the completed basket, leaving the village at dawn. As they come to the river, they respectfully place the basket into the water and patiently wait. This is their invitation to the fish to come to the basket. Not all days result in bringing fish to the village, for, on some days, such a response is not intended to occur. This is the lesson of patience and acceptance. The fisherman does not demand the fish to enter. He lives with the wisdom and understanding that much is not within his power. His strength is his gentleness and his willingness to allow the fish to come.

This knowledge takes many years and maturity to learn, appreciate, and perform. This is why he never performs this task alone but always with an apprentice. On the days when his basket holds fish, he carries the gift with gratitude to those whose tasks are at the fire of nourishment. In the days of abundance, they are grateful. Often, in times of plenty, they are jubilant as they enjoy the richness of the gifts. In the days of scarcity, they still remain grateful for the river, the fish, and the knowledge of the fisherman. Gratitude is not dependent on the outcome of the task. Gratitude is for opportunity, for possibility.

The Lesson of the Patient Gardener

Today, *the elders said*, we wish to impart upon you the lesson of the patient gardener. This lesson is not for you alone but to be shared with the parents, the teachers, the mentors, the employers, and all who touch the lives of developing children, adolescents, and young adults. In juxtaposition to the nurturing of a child and the enormous challenges, cares, and concerns of that awesome task, we present this lesson briefly and simplistically. We make this point in this manner to encourage the acceptance and practice of this concept and direction. Let us assist, as we create a gentle, seemingly simple, and yet substantial symbolic metaphor for guidance.

Just as the patient gardener stands before the trumpet vine in the early spring, in kind respect of what the intention of the vine is to be, this is how we must view, speak, and handle the children in our lives. Our mission is to remain in complete awe of the beauty and uniqueness before us. Just as the patient gardener does not unfairly request that the trumpet vine should become a hydrangea vine, when standing before the child, one must always honor the intention of what *the child is meant to be.*

When caring for children, ours is the job of the patient gardener who gently tends for many seasons. The task of the patient gardener is not to stand before the vine with a predetermined concept or a vision and then attempt to uncover that concept or vision in the vine. The growth of a child is not something to be created but observed and supported gently, as the vine is by the gardener. You must stop and remove your ego and your design in the springtime of their lives, as you wait patiently for them to emerge.

Charging forth with an ego-driven-will shall only result in the breaking of branches. The action of pruning too soon will only remove opportunity. You must stand back patiently as you ask, "What is the intention of what you shall be? I shall listen." Investigate how you can support what they are destined to become. Of course, providing shelter, water, and nourishment is necessary. But as they attempt to explore their possibilities, you must allow the fresh, fragile, young, vibrant new shoots to grow in varied directions, as you patiently wait for their conclusion. And you must understand that, if the vine is intended to grow over the trellis, the vine shall do so. Your task is to provide the trellis. Provide *many* trellises! Your job is to support their varying explorations through many seasons, without judgment of the outcome. Remind yourself that there are many avenues that lead to growth and flourishing. Oftentimes, the vine growing quietly beneath the earth is the one that, when ready, emerges to become the strongest, growing over the trellis and becoming rich with multitudes of blossoms.

Again, as the gardener does when tending the vines, protect the children from the storms as you are able to do so. And when you cannot, come to their aid and offer healing, safety, and comfort. Remind yourself that each breeze they will face head-on will be coming to them for the first time. They have never been present on that day, at that age, with that particular wind. Please be aware that the winds shift and alter direction over generations, so also be reminded that your own survival is from storms you weathered in years past. The methods you used at that time, although successful, may not apply to the storms of these days.

Please remember at all times that no vine is unworthy, and no two vines are identical. All vines—all souls—come from spirit, the highest source, or God, and, therefore, all are as intended. If your task is done well, someday you shall have the magnificent privilege of standing back in awe, with joy in your heart, as you privately understand that nothing is more beautiful than a well-tended vine. Please, honor us by being the patient gardener.

The Lesson of Passing Over

With my sincere gratitude, this entry is dedicated to the memory of Lynn Obermiller, who so very generously allowed me the privilege of sitting alongside her as she courageously, faithfully—and with unfathomable love, kindness, and graciousness—passed over.

When I returned to the village, the elders greeted me with a solemn declaration. You have now been granted the privilege of observing the process of passing over. You were brought to this lesson with purpose and intention. You have witnessed—and you now understand—the beauty of this natural event and the gentle peace brought to the soul of the one passing over. You were able to observe the incomprehensible joy and, within that, the absence of fear or regret. All thoughts of the physical life that had been lived, and the emotions connected to all aspects of that life, were released. You watched as the soul, which was no longer earthbound, became part of the soaring heavens.

Those who are traveling their paths upon earth have great difficulty understanding the complete release of everything they have ever understood. You see, the process of passing over is not of the Earth but of the Heavens. Earthly thoughts and logic no longer exist. Those who find discomfort in the concept of passing over are viewing the event within the realm of the physical world. Peace and acceptance are available to them should they make every attempt to envision this process as one of the soul. This is the soul's opportunity to experience freedom from the bondage of a physical lifetime, which has been lived to the intended conclusion. No matter when this occurs, the timing is appropriate. There are no accidents in the departure of a soul from the physical world.

As you witnessed, there exists a brief, fleeting moment, as the soul passes over, when there is an awareness of both worlds, as if the person is standing in a doorway of the universe, with one foot upon each side. This is a momentary time of reflection, of letting go, saying farewell, and being granted the grace of acceptance. Passing over is the joyous homecoming of the soul.

We invited you to witness the moment of freedom that the soul experiences. Was there anything more beautiful? Ahhhh. We kindly smile, as we see that your thoughts have created a comparison—to birth. Yes, we agree. Birth is awe-inspiring. However, we ask you to consider that even a birth can be set in circumstances filled with mixed emotions. Isn't there something bittersweet about a child being born amidst evidence that much of the path ahead for that child may hold many struggles and even pain? You see, all things of earth are subject to the ramifications, limits, and structures of the physical world. Birth is bound by earth. This is not true of death. The soul, returning home, is boundless, expansive beyond measure and beyond understanding. Death, you see, is not of the Earth, but of the Heavens. Do you now see that nothing is more beautiful than death? Not even birth, which you have perceived to be the most beautiful earth event?

We brought you to this lesson with purpose since many misunderstand death—the passing over. They have forgotten that this is a natural conclusion to a life lived. Death is as intended—a completion of a cycle, a journey, which has been decided upon, even chosen, prior to birth. After passing over, the soul is overjoyed, as you witnessed. There is no regret, pain, judgment, guilt, anger, or resentment—only bliss, in the purest form. Many live in fear of their own passing, and many more live their lives in regret and sadness over those who have passed. Through your written words, speak to those who are fearful, sad, or regretful so they might find peace. There are many who have already spoken of this. We ask you to bravely allow your voice to be added to the others. May your words, dear child, bring some measure of comfort.

The Lesson of Being Forever Connected

O*nce again, the elders spoke.* Take my hand, *they said in their collective voice*, for today we shall travel joined as partners, and for this time, we shall be as one. Allow my strength, my confidence, and my courage to flow from my heart into my hand as I offer all of those things to you. Let us interlace our fingers, creating a union of combined effort. In the joining of our two souls, you shall be assisted in your time of fear. As we walk along as one, feel the encouragement which comes to you. Do you notice how your struggles become less overwhelming? The rocks and pebbles which greet you become more and more manageable as we proceed.

At times, you will see the path narrow, appearing as though there is not enough room for us to walk side by side. But we do not let go. We adjust ourselves, as one of us momentarily takes the lead and the other follows. At other times, if one of us is unsure or hesitates, the other takes the lead. We alternate, according to that which comes before us, making the necessary adjustments appropriately. This journey that we travel together today is meant to symbolize the path we travel—the one we always share—with spirit, the highest source, or God.

We ask you to understand that, at all times, we are joined. We are interlaced with a source greater than ourselves. This is something we must remember, not only when we are fearful, but also when we are strong. Through all of our journeys upon the path we travel, we are forever connected. We must not let go. When we are triumphant, we are not independent in that success. The celebration is shared, for we are always entwined with spirit, the highest source, or God. Similarly, when we are in fear, filled with sorrow, or not physically or spiritually well, that connection always continues to exist. We are never abandoned.

As we journey upon our path, we may meet other travelers, love other travelers, and become in community with others. But ultimately, our path is only permanently connected to one, to that of spirit, the highest source, or God. Only in that union do we find that being alone is impossible. Let this serve to comfort you in those moments when you experience abandonment by humanity. Draw upon this knowledge in times of loss. Use this knowledge to give you strength and to keep you steadfast in your journey upon your path. Although you may feel alone, you are not.

As in the darkness, we ask that you do not feel alone. We ask that you be aware of this in moments of triumph as well. You must humble yourself and accept that your success is a shared victory. To ignore this is to be ego-driven, self-driven, and self-appointed as the highest source. This is living falsely. When we are fearful and even desolate, believing we are without hope is also living falsely. These opposing thoughts are elements of the same false belief—that you are the highest source. We ask that you remain mindful that the highest source is not within you but rather within spirit, the highest source, or God. Through that understanding, you will find honesty and integrity as you continue to seek your intended purpose for the highest good.

The Lesson of Release

On this day, *the elders announced*, we ask you to travel with us to the river where you will receive your lesson. This lesson shall become one of the most precious gifts you will receive. You will be taught the lesson of release, the gentle letting go and rinsing away. At the river, you may unburden your soul, as the waters carry away your worries, concerns, hurt, and, when necessary, your misdirected ego. There is much that is not within your power. Though you may have love in your heart, and good intention, grasping tightly prevents independence and freedom. You must allow for the right of all to practice self-will.

Through our life paths, we are brought to the opportunities for growth. The varying topographies of our lives become our teachers. Why do we see truth in the belief that our task is to direct our course, or those courses of others, when we do not create *any* of those paths? We invite you to come to the river today to wash away your burdens, to learn the lesson of release. Hidden beneath the river, within the bedrock, is where the very first drops of peace are born, as release gives birth to acceptance—and acceptance, dear child, is the parent of peace.

We four elders stand at the shore of the river in symbolic positions that serve as messages, as we direct you to this lesson. The first one of us standing on the far left, with arms outstretched toward the water, demonstrates that this is the place where you may wash your burdens away. Those burdens are many, and they weigh upon your heart too heavily. Remove hesitation from your steps and allow yourself freedom and release. Let go of your thoughts and concerns. Allow them to wash upon the waters of the river and float away. With trust and faith, be reminded that you are supported. Rest. Float peacefully upon the waters of love, protection, and support from the universe. Allow your plans to be carried away and released, for you are not the creator. Tiny ebbs of rippling waters wash over you as they float away your concerns, pain, and hurt. Profound faith is experienced in the process of letting go, in recognizing that there is one larger than self, more knowing and everlasting. The path you travel, and the paths of those your life has touched, have not been created by you. Although you may contribute actions, the course has ultimately been directed from above. All is by design.

Next to the first elder stands the second, with arms outstretched. This is the symbol of eternal welcome, for all are welcome, at all times. No burden brought upon you by others or by self is too great. No deed or concern exists that cannot be washed away, no matter the action, intent, or thought. The waters of this river are continually replenished and are incapable of being muddied. Even the greatest of your burdens, the darkest of your stories, or the deepest of your shame will be washed away. Within this river, there is no judgment—only the waters of rejuvenation.

Between the two elders on the left and the two who stand on the right there exists a space. This serves to represents that there is always an opening for you to enter. Come, as we support your steps. You are not alone. You will not drown. You are weary and have traveled far. You are home. You are safe.

To the right of the opening stands the third elder, arms outstretched toward the sky, for spirit, the highest source, or God, is with us. This is how the stream is fed. We feel joy, for spirit, the highest source, or God, will lighten our burdens. Allow your heart to drink the waters and replenish your soul as you become a renewed vessel to hold love. Relax your body. You need not work. Instead, float effortlessly, motionlessly. Be still, for the waters will lift you, raise you, and support you.

To the right, the fourth and final elder stands with arms in a self-embrace, hands resting upon the heart. This is to remind you that you are loved and that we hold you to our heart. If you should come brokenhearted, with sadness and grief weighing heavily upon you, then that is how you shall come. Run, if you must. Crawl, if you must. You are loved without judgment, no matter your condition. This elder is also there to remind you that your duty is to protect yourself. When you practice self-care and self-love, you are assisting us with our work. Use gentleness toward yourself, for you are never without our love. Though your path may bring you to times of loneliness, with or without others around you, you are never truly alone, for we are with you.

This river is yours to visit whenever you need to do so. When you visit, there will be no limits, no boundaries, no rules.

The river flows continuously, and the shore rests within your reach at all times. Do not become a stranger to the river, for without frequent washing away, the weight of your humanity can become too great, and there is no need to travel with those burdens. The river is ever-waiting. Please come often. As you enter the waters of the river, together we will lift your soul and lighten your load, and you will become buoyant with the love of spirit, the highest source, or God.

Lessons Completed

The elders spoke for what would turn out to be the last time in this portion of my journey. You come to us with an open and trusting heart and an eagerness to learn as you have been directed. We are very pleased at your progress, and we have enjoyed this portion of your journey with us. We have shared with you our insights, our wisdom, and the lessons appropriate for you at this time. For now, your lessons are complete. Do not feel sadness or disappointment. Our work together has only just begun. You now have an assignment, which must be fulfilled. This is your responsibility. You must prepare these lessons in a format that will enable them to be shared with others.

Do you see, child? We have traveled full circle. This ending delivers you to where you first began. You now stand once again at the beginning of your awareness of our journey together, at that first point when you wrote the words, "And I knew the time had come—to answer my spirit and have the courage to be misunderstood." The challenge before you is no longer "to answer my spirit," since that has been accomplished. Now the task before you is to "have the courage to be misunderstood." This is your call to service, and you may not do this privately. This portion of your journey will involve exposure to others and, ultimately, to the judgment of others.

You have resided within your studies in privacy, in the protective comfort of our company, where judgment does not exist. You must now venture outward, toward humanity, where there are many things of which we have spoken. With humanity comes the possibility of judgment, criticism, anger, jealousy, greed, resentment, and misunderstanding. We know you fear exposure, and we believe you have come to a point of self-acceptance and self-love that will enable you to withstand this risk. Your strength has grown, and you understand the lessons you have been given. These lessons now reside within you. They are an integral part of your soul, the soul that gave birth to the paintings of the trumpet vine, which were your physical expressions of our gift to you.

The time for completion has arrived. Do not delay or postpone in fear of the unknown ahead. We ask that you prepare the lessons, for the time is now. As promised, we will carve a path for you to be able to share them. We sense your fear and your lack of confidence in your own knowledge and practice of the lessons, as you still struggle on many days. Your expectations were inaccurate. You believed these lessons, once learned, would end your moments and days of misguided thoughts or actions. That is not their purpose. These lessons are not for learning and moving forward. No, they require the gentle practice, repeatedly, over and over. These lessons are meant to ebb and flow throughout your lifetime, to be called upon when needed. Let them become your first breath when you awaken and what you exhale as you close your eyes to rest. A well-lived life is one that requires self-observation on a daily basis. Using self-honesty and a willingness to continually grow, these lessons are a means to do that, as they are to be revisited again and again.

You and all the others who learn the lessons must understand they are not learned once and then abandoned. The lessons are to become the seeking, the intention of one's actions. True value is found, at times, when the lessons are executed beautifully. At other times, their value is understood only in reflection of the opposite behavior. This is why the value can never be placed solely upon the behavior of humanity.

The great potential of grasping the meaning of a successful life exists within this structure. The skill of *true mastery* is the ability to utilize that which you have learned while you continue to encounter challenges. Remember, as you gain confidence, that this does not indicate a life without struggle. The conflicts that accompanied you into this lifetime are the same ones that will depart with you. Mastery lies in the adept management of life's events between those two points in time.

Do not fret, child. With our most steadfast love, we offer these lessons to you. Take them. Come to understand them, again and again, as you gently practice them all of your days. Do not let them become a source to scold or punish yourself. Do not seek perfection. Just seek. Become one who risks self-observation and who facilitates changes within. For all days, continually deepen your understanding of the lessons. Through that practice you shall experience peace. This, child, is the mastery of a lifetime.

Afterword

The time had come for me to step away from my writing desk, to pause, to embrace the concept of completion. With a sigh, my hands dropped to my sides. Their work, perhaps only briefly, was finished. My hands had served as the legs that had carried me along this path. The steps, the hills, and the valleys I had traveled—the difficult climbs and painful backward slides—had taken place one letter at a time on my keyboard. I held my hands in front of me for examination. I wondered if they could answer the question: "Has there been purpose?"

My hands were older than I had planned. That was absolutely for certain. I had never imagined the work they would need to do. I could not have fathomed the soil I would have to dig into nor the rocks I would need to cling to, at times, as I grasped for life. Nor could I have imagined the immense joy they would experience—the babies they would hold or the tears they would be able to wipe away for those children, if only for a short time. Little children had grown into young adults, and my hands had lost their power. Maybe my words could become a way to assist them on their own journeys.

Inconceivable was the pain these hands would need to carry while I was on my journey of self-discovery. And that was probably best, while I was also learning to accept the circumstances embedded in the distance I had traveled. I never thought to consider the number of hands I would need to reach for in desperation. When I began, I believed all journeys were made alone. I was only partially accurate. I would have never guessed which hands would be the ones that reached back to me, or the hurt I would experience from the ones that did not. Yet I thanked them. I thanked them all.

I stood up from my desk, in my little writing cottage at Rooster Ridge. And as I stepped back, I viewed the canvases of the trumpet vine, shaking my head in disbelief at myself. *Twelve* paintings? I couldn't have painted just *one*? Obviously not. Side by side, they were twelve feet long and nine feet tall. What a leap of faith that was, and still is, in my estimation! I loved those paintings. I was happy I'd taken that leap—moving furniture, nailing the heavy cotton drop cloth to the wall, adding more nail holes to hold those canvases than any wall should have ever had to bear. I struggled, at times, in front of the puzzled look on the teenagers' faces that entered and exited as they passed through on their way to their next adventure. I was following my passion, working toward a vision that I had. Maybe I made it easier for them to do the same. I think I did.

I surveyed my environment as a new observer. Things made more sense now. My eyes fell upon the multitudes of various depictions of roosters—everywhere roosters: proud painted images, ceramic statues with chests puffed up preparing to crow, a poster of Picasso's rooster, sculpted iron that had been melded into crowing beaks and majestic tail feathers. Plates, cups and bowls, napkins and pillows. Roosters. Carved wooden roosters flanking each doorway. Now I understood my attraction to them, the way they called to me—the message to begin another day, to draw forth every ounce of life force I could muster and crow. I hoped I had crowed well.

On top of the pine armoire was the collection of bowls—the symbol of humanity. Dried pieces of Sycamore bark and feathers gathered from the ground—the invitation. The words I had written ten years before and painted on the handmade tablecloth now made sense—"answer your spirit" and "the courage to be misunderstood." And outside the windows, trumpet vines grew.

I smiled to myself, to my hands. I smiled as well to the elders in their village. I had come to know and love them, and I hoped that more of them awaited me.

Then I heard the elders softly speak in gentle reassurance, Yes, dear child, *they said to me*, more awaits. For we shall accompany you as you now make your way to courageously speak of another journey you made, the one into the canyon.

Acknowledgments

I am so very grateful to so many who have traveled before me and alongside me; they have become my teachers, my mentors, my guides, my examples, and my inspiration. They have often become my friends and loved ones as well. With gratitude, I wish to acknowledge some of *the hands that reached back*.

To my *four corners*—Courage, Acceptance, Wisdom, and Love.

To Kimberly Couri, who served as the inspiration for me to become courageous.

To Jake Couri, who, through his own gifts, granted me the grace of acceptance.

To Patricia McGuire, who generously shared her insight, knowledge, and wisdom. Thank you for your patience and your belief in me, and for demonstrating, through those, that I was worth the effort.

To Steven Cohen, who lovingly stepped into my life and answered my heartfelt prayer that said, "I want to be cherished." I am so very fortunate to be loved by you.

To Jinny Joy Johnson—Thank you for your spiritual mentoring and for teaching me and sharing with me your understanding of *spirit*. You share your incredible wisdom so lovingly and generously, and I am so grateful. Thank you for your love and friendship.

To Lisa Mahmarian Strouth, for teaching me what being an artist means, for graciously sharing your experience and knowledge, and for explaining to me that I, too, am an artist. Thank you.

To Cheri Laser, for providing me with your excellent editing skills and for your willingness to so generously share your experience and knowledge with me. You appeared in my life so effortlessly at a Memorial Day parade and moved me through the process so graciously. I am indebted to you always.

To Stephanie Violette—Thank you for allowing your professional, artistic, and skillful photography to be a part of this experience. Interacting with you is always a pleasure as you participate so very joyfully.

To Bob Couri, who, through his success and dedicated work ethic, provided me the resources to be able to heal myself and to experience the incredible privilege of devoting my time to our children.

To Nancy Cohen—Thank you for sharing with me the story of your own journey as I was attempting to understand mine.

To Sandy Rousso—Thank you for sharing your healing energy, your trustworthiness, and your insight with me.

To Mike Metchikin, for teaching me that I could be strong.

To Rick Cyriacks, for sharing with me the wonderful person you are, for your kindness, and for sharing your Sycamore bark.

To Dee Ellison, who, for years and unbeknownst to me, included me in her prayers.

And to Patti Jean Obermiller, for always being my friend.

CPSIA information can be obtained
at www.ICGtesting.com
Printed in the USA
LVIC05n0123230215
427911LV00001B/1

* 9 7 8 1 4 5 7 5 0 5 5 9 1 *